THE UN[...]

FOX-HUNTING

BY

C. F. P. McNEILL, M.F.H.

WITH INTRODUCTION BY

HIS GRACE THE DUKE OF BEAUFORT

NOTES ON THE USE OF THE
HORN AND THE WHISTLE
AND LIST OF FIVE THOUSAND
NAMES OF HOUNDS . . .

PRICE 5/- NET.

LONDON :
VINTON & CO., LTD.,
8, BREAM'S BUILDINGS, CHANCERY LANE, E.C.

TO

HIS GRACE THE DUKE OF BEAUFORT

THESE FEW LINES ON

"THE UNWRITTEN LAWS OF FOX-HUNTING"

ARE

Dedicated

IN THE HOPE THAT THEY MAY BE OF SOME SLIGHT
USE TO THOSE TAKING FOX-HOUNDS
FOR THE FIRST TIME.

C. F. P. McNEILL.

INTRODUCTORY

BY

HIS GRACE THE DUKE OF BEAUFORT.

THE Author of this pamphlet conceived the idea of putting in tangible form the previously un-written laws of Fox-hunting, and sent them to me to peruse. This I have done with great interest and pleasure. I have made several suggestions and slight alterations, which have been carried out, and I think and hope, with the Author, that they may be of use to those gentlemen who are taking or contemplating taking hounds for the first time. It has often struck me, as it has struck others, that there is a lamentable amount of ignorance amongst those who hunt with regard to what you may do and what you may not do out hunting. This little treatise seems to me just to hit the vital points without diving into a subject that bristles with interest.

The Author has evidently had no idea of making a book up with padding. The simple facts are stated and left alone, and I hope with him that it may save many a hunting squabble, which is always to be regretted, particularly when connected with the "Noble Science."

BEAUFORT.

BADMINTON,
     GLOS.

CONTENTS

The Unwritten Laws of Fox-Hunting

(*a*) If a pack of hounds should run a fox over their border into a neighbouring country and he should get to ground, the Master of the invading pack has a perfect right to get him out in the following ways; but he must under no circumstances use a spade or pickaxe, or break soil or turf in any way *whatever*.

1. He may put a terrier in, provided he belongs to his Hunt establishment, and is either running with the pack, or carried by a second horseman, or terrier boy or runner. He must not commandeer a terrier out of his country or in the country into which he runs.

2. He may try and swill the fox out.

3. He may use a pole and try to poke him out.

4. He may use a squib and try to smoke him out.

If there is more than one fox in the hole or drain, he only has a right to kill one. Cecil says on page 43 of his 'Words of the Chase,'

" A fox may be bolted by a terrier provided the terrier belongs to the Master of the hounds and is therefore with them, but it is held inadmissible to borrow a dog for the occasion. This is certainly a very punctilious action, but it is one for which there is a precedent, and the propriety of it has been admitted."

(*b*) If a pack of hounds should run a fox over their border into a neighbouring country and apparently lose him, and eventually turn to go back into their own domains, and a fox is holloa'd at no great distance from where they lost their fox, they have a perfect right to go and hunt that fox, as it is impossible to say it was not their hunted fox who had lain down ; but, supposing they had trotted, say two miles or so from where the fox had been lost and then a holloa occurred, or information came to hand of a fox having been seen, the huntsman should not lay his hounds on, for it is not a good sportsman who poaches ; and this rule, of course, must be somewhat elastic and left to the sportsmanlike instincts of Masters and huntsmen ; but I should think any distance like the one mentioned would under ordinary circumstances quite preclude hounds being laid on. If a fox jumps up when hounds are running outside

their own country and hounds chopped him by
accident, you would have perfect right to go on
with the hunted fox, or if you had run five
miles over the border of your country and had
trotted back to within two fields or a few
hundred yards of your boundary and a fox was
holloa'd, it would undoubtedly not be strictly
orthodox to lay hounds on over your border ;
but supposing the fox had actually come out
of your country and you chose to take hounds
those few fields back so as to be in your own
territory when you first strike the line, of course
you could follow him anywhere.

In cub-hunting you should keep as much as
possible to your own country, and certainly so
during September. In October, when hounds
are let go, it is more difficult to do so, but it
is annoying to a Master to have a neighbouring
pack running a fox into a nice sized covert with
a strong litter of cubs, where he himself was
contemplating a good morning a few days later.
Though there is no rule about this, and as a
Master has a perfect right to take a cub over
his border into a covert, small or large, of his
neighbours, and try to kill him in any way
he can, except by use of spade or pick as
mentioned previously, it is better to keep to

your own country till later on ; besides, for the reasons already mentioned, farmers must be considered, and fat cattle have not yet been turned into bank notes, and being galloped about does not tend to put more weight on them. Therefore orthodox cub-hunting is best left till the middle of October, at least.

(c) A new-comer into a country should at once inform the Secretary of the Hunt, so that all circulars and notices may be sent to him. He should inquire what subscriptions would be satisfactory for him to give, if there is no rule laid down by the Hunt Committee, and also if a Poultry Fund, and should send his cheque at once, and write a note asking if the Master has any objection to his coming out cub-hunting. The Master will, of course, answer the letter in a gracious manner, saying how pleased he will be to see him.   He will, however, be very careful not to stand about coffee-housing on the rides, or to bring out a kicking horse.

(d) When hounds are trotting on to draw, the huntsman's attention is often taken up by gentlemen trotting up to talk to him.   No one should speak to a huntsman without first riding up to the Master and getting his permission to do so ; but the less a huntsman is spoken to the

more time he will have to attend to the business
in hand.

(*e*) It does not seem to be generally understood now, as it was in the old days, that cub-
hunting is entirely a private matter, and no
business of anyone's but the Master's, to educate
his entry and educate his foxes—anyone coming
out comes out on sufferance. It must be left
entirely to the discretion of the Master how
many cubs he thinks it advisable to kill, etc.,
also whether he sends cards of these meets
out or not, and at what hour he decides to
meet.

(*f*) As regards neutral countries, no absolute
rule is applicable which would suit them all,
the local neutrality being generally fixed by
the two Hunt Committees concerned. Any
dispute arising should be reported to the M.F.H.
Association. Some countries have a portion
that is drawn by two different packs, taking
months and months about; other neutral por-
tions are drawn just as it suits these packs, and
so on.

(*g*) As regards the "walking" of foxhound
puppies outside the boundary of a Hunt, this
has often led to great unpleasantness. I think
that a gentleman, be he farmer or millionaire,

who lives on or near the boundary of two Hunts and subscribes to both, has a perfect right to take a puppy from each Master, but he should not take one from the Master whose country he is just outside of, and refuse to take one from his own Master. In other words, every one walking a puppy for a neighbouring Hunt should at least offer to take one from his own Hunt too, otherwise the practice is open to question.

(*h*) Gentlemen should come to the meet and not anticipate the draw.

(*i*) There is no class of person who gets a Hunt into disrepute more than second horsemen. These, as a rule, are stable helpers dressed up in livery, extremely thoughtless, and noted for leaving gates open and very often jumping their masters' horses over fences. The strictest orders possible should be given to them, not once, but several times during the season.

(*j*) As regards those who come out cub-hunting, I cannot do better than quote Lord Willoughby de Broke's excellent letter to the editor of 'Horse and Hound' on September 8th, 1910, and I am quite sure he will forgive me for doing so. I give it verbatim, and no one will do wrong if they follow it out :—" May

I appeal to those who wish to see the Warwick-
shire Hounds at work during the cub-hunting
season to make the huntsman's task as easy as
possible, and at the same time to reduce to its
narrowest limits the risk of kicking hounds ?

"These objects can be helped in two ways:—

" 1st. By keeping outside the coverts.

" This will give the huntsman and staff the
fullest opportunity of serving the pack, as
well as of viewing foxes crossing the rides.
It will also save a great many accidents to
hounds.

" 2nd. By not allowing grooms to come out
cub-hunting.

"Any horse is liable to kick a hound, but
especially at this time of year, when horses are
fresh and hounds are constantly emerging from
the covert unexpectedly to join the cry of the
other hounds.

" I write rather feelingly, as I have just had
a valuable hound badly kicked.

" I feel quite confident, however, that ladies
and gentlemen will realise how very materially
they can contribute to the success of cub-
hunting by falling in with these two simple
requests."

(k) As to the moving of cubs, this is always

a very doubtful policy, as cubs rarely do any good when transferred from one part of the country to the other. If a complaint is made to the Master as regards a litter being in too close proximity to a hen roost, it is better to send the huntsman to burn some sulphur in the holes, and the vixen is certain to shift them that night. Care must be taken not to overdo it and thereby smother the cubs. As regards cubs in a boundary fence adjoining a neighbouring hunt, or even near the boundary of another hunt, these should under no circumstances be tampered with by a Master unless he is in complete accord with the neighbouring Master, as he, for instance, may have a covert close to, where he is expecting these cubs to shift into, or they may, in fact, have been originally laid down there, and made a shift over the boundary for a week or two. It would therefore be a most unneighbourly action to move them, besides being absolutely against the rules and usages of fox-hunting.

(*l*) A Master of a pack of hounds, whether a subscription pack or carried on entirely at his own expense, has *undoubtedly* a perfect right to take hounds home whenever he wishes. He is absolute master. The country is handed over to him to hunt to the best of his ability, and if he for any reason considers the interests of the Hunt will be furthered by his taking the hounds home, he can do so for any cause whatever, either over riding hounds, riding over crops, or any want of discipline, or any other reason, though, of course, it is better to send the offender home than take the extreme measure, which spoils a day's sport for many innocent people.

(m) In countries where there is shooting, a Master should write to each covert owner and ask him to kindly furnish the dates on which he intends to shoot, so that he may keep hounds out for the days previously, and also whether he would like the hounds to come and cub-hunt his coverts. One sport should never be carried on to the detriment of another, and it must be remembered there is no better sportsman than he who preserves foxes, though he is not a hunting man himself, and should have every consideration.

(n) The question of advertising meets has often arisen, particularly in the shires, where an enormous crowd has to be dealt with. I may state at once this is entirely at the Master's discretion. Means, of course (presumably by

C

card), will be taken to acquaint subscribers of the fixtures. I am talking of meets after November 1st, as I dealt with this matter as regards cub-hunting in paragraph (*e*).

(*o*) In some countries the hounds belong to trustees, having either been purchased by the country or presented to the country. In this case an incoming Master takes over a certain number, and is bound to leave the same number on his retirement, of sound working hounds.

(*p*) On or before February 1st in each year all Masters wishing to resign should acquaint the Chairman of the Hunt Committee or the Secretary, so as to give the country a chance of securing the services of the best Master possible ; also it is only fair to the Hunt servants to be given as long as possible to obtain situations. After February 1st, no notice having been received by a Committee, they are justified in presuming the Master intends going on for another season.

(*q*) There is a Freemasonry amongst Masters of Hounds in allowing each other the free use of any hound in their kennel for Stud purposes. No Master ever charges a Stud fee. The practice being for a Master to send the huntsman a tip for any trouble he may have been put to in

the matter.   The last few years some huntsmen
have rather tried to lay down a law and charge
10s. per head per bitch sent, and also 2s. or
2s. 6d. for their kennelman.   This is altogether
an innovation, and when a stereotyped bill is
made out, and that amount *demanded*, it prac-
tically amounts to a Stud fee.   Also if a Master
uses one kennel exclusively, and sends as many
as thirty or forty couples of bitches to that
kennel, it becomes a serious item, if he has to
send the huntsmen £30 or £40, a perquisite
out of all proportion, particularly if a large
percentage of these bitches miss.   The Master
pays, has few whelps, and loses a whole year.
Masters, of course, allow their huntsmen to take
what is given or sent as a tip ; but they should
strongly set their face against a tariff per bitch
being made out, and sent in the form of a bill,
and payment demanded, as this does away with
all the old usages and the unwritten law of
Fox-hunting.   If a Master sent the huntsman,
whose stallion hound he uses, 10s. per head for
every bitch in whelp, it would then amount
to a very handsome present, and an enormous
perquisite in kennels where blood is much
sought after.   In any case, the expense of
sending bitches from one end of England to the

other, very often in charge of a whipper-in, is of itself a great expense, and in many cases the kennel is a long way from a Railway Station, and more expense is incurred. Foxhound sires *always* have been and *always* should be free, and the huntsman's tips must be *entirely gratuitous*. I write this after consulting several authorities, who were very strong on the subject, and I am sure it is right, and the wish of most Masters of Foxhounds.

The Dukes of Beaufort, for all time, have been considered the great authorities on the unwritten laws of fox-hunting, and have each in turn settled many disputes that have threatened to grow to large proportions. The present Duke of Beaufort's knowledge of the noble sport is second to none, and his well thought out and tactful decisions have saved many a dispute from being taken to the M.F.H. Association. In other words, he is always ready to sit as a judge in chambers, and give his valuable opinion in the interests of Fox-hunting.

THE HORN

IT is essential that every note blown on the horn should have a meaning, otherwise neither the Field nor the Whippers-in know what is going on. Some Huntsmen blow at random, any note just as it suits their lip. Tom Firr never deceived his hounds, never deceived his Field, everyone knew the particular notes he blew as well as if he was speaking. When drawing a Woodland, a Huntsman should blow *one note* on his horn, occasionally, to keep hounds from getting too wide. Such a note is no signal for the Whippers-in to turn, put on, nor rate hounds. If, however, the note is repeated three or four times, the Huntsman probably requires a Whip's presence, either for riot or to rate hounds for picking up trash, etc. Two or three quick notes on the horn mean "a fox is on foot," and if any hounds are near a Whipper-in, he may encourage them to get together with "Hoic! Hoic! Hoic!" This cheer should not be given in such a way as to drown the challenge of the hounds on the line, nor in such a way as to make hounds that are further off think it is a " View holloa."

The " Gone away " is a succession of sharp notes on the horn which is unmistakable.

The " View holloa" should never be used except when a fox is first viewed over a ride when drawing a cover, or in holloaing a fox away from a cover, but it should then be immediately followed by " Forward, away, away, away, away ! " Under *no circumstances* whatever should a "View holloa" be used *in cover*, when hounds are bringing a good line to the person who has viewed the fox. Such a holloa then only tends to get the hounds' heads up and defeats the object for which it was intended, viz., to get nearer the fox. " Tally ho over ! " when a fox crosses a ride is quite sufficient, except in a big Woodland, when hounds are at fault a long way off, then a " View holloa," delivered twice or three times, will bring the Huntsman at once to the spot. This of course does not apply to a sinking fox and a tired pack of hounds, when a good cheery halloa rams the hounds together, and when close to their fox, makes the pack run keener and get together.

The Field should never holloa or attempt to make hunting noises when any of the servants are there. Nothing is so pleasing as a really good "View holloa," nothing so discordant as a bad one, or two people holloaing at the same time. All other cries should be very distinctive —for instance, a fox is viewed away, but before he has gone a field he is headed or changes his mind. *No* "View holloa" should be given, simply "Tally ho, back!" as otherwise if a "View holloa" were given, the pack would come tumbling out of the cover with their heads up : with the greatest difficulty they would be stopped, turned back into cover and got to put their heads down again, much valuable time being lost, besides deceiving the Huntsman, who, but for this, would have had an eye down a ride back, and very likely have viewed the fox and been able to get the pack close on to him. It must always be remembered that all holloas are for the information of the Huntsman and his attendants. No holloa of any sort should be given until you arrive at the *exact* spot where the fox has been seen, either in holloaing a fox away, or in holloaing a fox over a ride.

THE WHISTLE

A WHISTLE is the greatest boon to Master, Servants, and Field alike in any country. Lord Lonsdale used it with the Quorn, and it was of the greatest success, as much so as it is in the Duke of Beaufort's big Woodlands. It should be blown on *one* occasion and on *one* occasion *only*, and that is—when a fox has gone away. A holloa means *nothing*, a yokel holloas because he has seen a fox on the opposite hillside, or he saw a fox come back into the wood; but if a Huntsman hears the well-known whistle he knows it is one of his own servants, and above all he knows it is right, and gets there as quickly as possible. Hounds soon learn it and it is surprising to see how they fly to it. The Huntsman arriving at the place where the fox has " gone away " joins in with the quick rattle on his horn, and as the pack settle on the line closely followed by the Huntsman and First Whip, the Second Whip lingers a few minutes longer still blowing his whistle to help the

delinquents out of their difficulty, and let the
stragglers know the pack's away. It is far
better than holloaing behind a pack, as you so
often see, the consequence being that if scent is
bad and they check a few fields further on, and
hear the holloa behind them, they stand about
and star-gaze, and I have seen them start to go
back, thinking it right.

It should never be forgotten that all signals
out hunting should be plainly understood by the
Staff. Without a perfect understanding between
the Huntsman and Whips confusion will ensue
and sport suffer. When viewing a fox over a
ride, always turn the horse's head the way the
fox has gone, pointing out some mark, such as
a tree or a bush, to show exactly where he has
crossed. It should be remembered that when a
fox hears a holloa over a ride, he frequently
recrosses a few yards lower down, and so, should
the head be turned away when holloaing, the
fox may escape notice and a great loss of time
ensue.

D

HOUND NAMES

The following List of Hound Names are given by the kind permission of the Author.

Abbess
Abbot
Abdicant
Abdicate
Abelard
Abercorn
Abigail
Absolom
Absolute
Accent
Accident
Accurate
Acheron
Acid
Acklam
Ackland
Ackworth
Acme
Acolyte
Aconite
Acorn
Acrobat
Active
Acton
Actor
Actress
Actual
Ada
Adamant
Adequate
Adela
Adelaide
Adeline

Adjective
Adjutant
Admiral
Adrian
Advent
Advocate
Affable
Affluent
Afghan
African
Agatha
Agent
Agile
Agnes
Agony
Aide-de-
      camp
Aider
Ailsa
Aimless
Aimwell
Ainsworth
Airlie
Airy
Ajax
Akbar
Akerman
Alaric
Albany
Albemarle
Albert
Albion
Alderman

Alfred
Alias
Alibi
Alice
Alien
Aliment
Alistair
Allspice
Alma
Almoner
Alpha
Alphabet
Alpine
Altitude
Alto
Amabel
Amazon
Amber
Ambrose
Ambush
Amersham
Amethyst
Amiable
Amity
Amnesty
Amorous
Amphora
Amulet
Amy
Analyst
Anarchist
Ancestor
Anchor

Anchorite
Andover
Anecdote
Angela
Angler
Anglesea
Angry
Anguish
Animate
Anna
Annabel
Anodyne
Answer
Antelope
Anthem
Anthony
Antic
Antidote
Antrim
Anxious
Apathy
Apple
Applicant
Approbate
Apricot
April
Apron
Aptitude
Arabi
Arbiter
Archer
Archibald
Architect

Arctic
Ardent
Arduous
Argent
Argonaut
Argosy
Argument
Argus
Ariel
Arklow
Armlet
Armourer
Arnica
Arrogant
Arsenal
Arsenic
Arson
Artemis
Artery
Artful
Arthur
Article
Artifice
Artist
Artless
Aspect
Asphodel
Aster
Asteroid
Atheist
Atlas
Attic
Attica

Attila
Attribute
Auburn
Audible
Audience
Auditor
Audrey
Augur
August
Augury
Auspice
Auster
Austral
Author
Authoress
Autocrat
Ava
Avarice
Average
Averil
Awful
Axiom
Ayah
Azure

Babbler
Baccarat
Bacchus
Bachelor
Badger
Baffler
Bagpipe
Bailiff
Bajazet
Baker
Balance
Ballad
Balmy
Balsam
Baltic
Bandage
Bandbox
Bandit

Bandy
Baneful
Bangle
Bangor
Banish
Banjo
Banker
Bankrupt
Banner
Banquet
Bantam
Banter
Bantling
Bantry
Barbara
Barber
Barbican
Bardolph
Barefoot
Barford
Bargain
Barleycorn
Barmaid
Barnaby
Barnard
Baroness
Baronet
Barrier
Barrister
Barter
Barton
Barstone
Bashful
Basil
Basilisk
Bathsheba
Battery
Battleaxe
Battler
Bauble
Bayard
Bayonet
Beacon
Beadle

Beadsman
Beaker
Bearer
Beatrice
Beaufort
Beauly
Beauteous
Beauty
Beckford
Bedford
Bedlam
Bedouin
Beeswing
Belford
Belfry
Bella
Bellflower
Bellmaid
Bellman
Belmont
Belvoir
Bencher
Bender
Bendigo
Benedict
Benefice
Benefit
Benison
Benjamin
Bentinck
Beresford
Bergamot
Berkeley
Bernard
Bertha
Bertram
Beryl
Bessemer
Bessy
Betsy
Beverley
Bilberry
Billesden
Billingsgate

Billow
Binder
Birdie
Birthday
Biscuit
Bishop
Bismarck
Bittern
Bitterness
Bivouac
Blackberry
Blackcap
Blackcock
Blackleg
Blacksmith
Blameless
Blandish
Blankney
Blarney
Blatant
Blazer
Blazon
Blenheim
Blemish
Blessing
Blissful
Blithesome
Bloomer
Blooming
Bloomy
Blossom
Blowsy
Blucher
Bluebeard
Bluebell
Bluecap
Blueskin
Blunder
Bluster
Boaster
Boastful
Bobadil
Bodkin
Boisterous

Bogie
Bolero
Bolingbroke
Bolster
Bolter
Bona
Bondage
Bondmaid
Bondsman
Bonfire
Bonniface
Bonnilass
Bonnybell
Bonnyfield
Bonus
Bootless
Booty
Borax
Boreas
Borderer
Boscabel
Bosphorus
Botany
Bouncer
Boundary
Boundless
Bounteous
Bounty
Bowler
Bowman
Bowsprit
Boxer
Boycott
Bracelet
Bracken
Bracket
Brackley
Bradshaw
Braggart
Bragger
Brakesman
Bramble
Brandy
Brasier

Bravery	Bumpkin	Cambric	Cartridge	Champion
Bravo	Bumptious	Cambridge	Carver	Chancellor
Brawler	Buoyant	Camelot	Casement	Chancery
Brazen	Burghley	Camera	Casket	Chandler
Breaker	Burglar	Cameron	Caspian	Changeable
Brecon	Burgundy	Camphor	Cassock	Chanter
Breezy	Burlington	Candid	Castanet	Chanticleer
Brenda	Burly	Candidate	Castaway	Chantress
Brennus	Burnish	Candle	Castor	Chantry
Brevity	Burnisher	Candour	Casual	Chaplain
Brewster	Bursar	Candy	Catapult	Chaplet
Bribery	Busby	Cannibal	Cataract	Chapman
Bridegroom	Bushman	Cannon	Caterer	Chapter
Bridesmaid	Bustler	Canopy	Catharine	Character
Bridget	Busy	Canticle	Cato	Charcoal
Briefless	Butterfly	Canvas	Cats'paw	Charger
Brigand	Buttress	Canvasser	Caudle	Charity
Brightness	Buxom	Capable	Causeway	Charlie
Brilliant	Buxton	Capital	Caustic	Charlotte
Brimstone	Buzzard	Capsicum	Cautious	Charmer
Briskly	Buzzer	Capsule	Cavernham	Charming
Bristol	Byeway	Captain	Cavity	Charon
Briton	Byron	Captious	Cecily	Charter
Brittle		Captive	Cedric	Chary
Broker		Capture	Celery	Chaser
Bruiser	Cabinet	Caradoc	Celia	Chastity
Brunswick	Cable	Caramel	Celtic	Chasuble
Brusher	Cackler	Carbine	Censor	Chatterbox
Bubbler	Cactus	Carbon	Census	Chatterer
Buckler	Cadence	Cardiff	Centaur	Chatty
Buckram	Cadger	Cardigan	Centipede	Checkmate
Buckshot	Cadmus	Cardinal	Cerberus	Cheddar
Buckthorn	Cæsar	Careful	Cereal	Cheeky
Buckwheat	Caitiff	Careless	Ceres	Cheerful
Budget	Caleb	Carlist	Certitude	Cheerily
Buffer	Calendar	Carmelite	Cestus	Cheery
Bugle	Caliban	Carmen	Chafer	Cherry
Bugler	Calico	Carnage	Chaffinch	Cherub
Builder	Caliph	Carnival	Chairman	Chickweed
Bullfinch	Callows	Carol	Chalky	Chicory
Bulrush	Calomel	Caroline	Challenger	Chieftain
Bulwark	Calmness	Carpenter	Chamberlain	Childeric
Bumble	Calmly	Carraway	Chamber-	Childish
Bumper	Calyx	Carrier	maid	Chilly

Chimer	Clematis	Columbine	Convoy	Cowslip
Chinaman	Clemency	Combat	Conway	Coxcomb
Chirper	Clencher	Comeaway	Copious	Coyly
Chocolate	Clerical	Comedy	Cora	Cracker
Chorister	Client	Comely	Coracle	Crackle
Chorus	Clifton	Comet	Coral	Cracknel
Christabel	Climax	Comfort	Cordage	Cracksman
Christian	Climbank	Comforter	Cordial	Cradle
Christmas	Clincher	Comical	Cordon	Craftsman
Chronicle	Clinical	Commerce	Corkscrew	Crafty
Chuckaway	Clinker	Commodore	Corky	Crammer
Chuckle	Clio	Commoner	Cormorant	Cranmer
Churlish	Clockwork	Compact	Cornet	Cranberry
Chutney	Cloister	Compass	Cornwall	Crasher
Cicely	Closure	Competent	Coroner	Craven
Cicero	Cloudy	Compliment	Coronet	Crazy
Cinder	Clover	Compton	Corporal	Credence
Cinnamon	Clumsy	Comrade	Corridor	Credible
Cipher	Cluster	Comus	Corsair	Credit
Circuit	Clydesdale	Concord	Corset	Creditor
Citizen	Coaster	Concourse	Corsican	Credulous
Citron	Coastguard	Concrete	Corydon	Creeper
Claimable	Coaxer	Condor	Cossack	Crescent
Claimant	Cobbler	Conscious	Costly	Cressida
Clamour	Cobnut	Conscript	Cosy	Cretonne
Clamorous	Cobweb	Conference	Cottager	Cribbage
Clansman	Cockney	Conflict	Counsellor	Cricketer
Clara	Cockroach	Congress	Countenance	Criminal
Clarence	Cockspur	Conical	Counter	Crimson
Clarendon	Cocktail	Conjuror	Counterfeit	Crinkle
Claret	Coddle	Conqueror	Counterpane	Crinoline
Claribel	Coddler	Conquest	Countess	Crisis
Clarion	Coinage	Conrad	Countless	Crispin
Clasher	Coiner	Consort	Countryman	Critic
Clasper	Colchester	Constable	Courier	Critical
Classic	Coldstream	Constance	Courser	Crochety
Classical	Colleague	Constant	Courteous	Crockery
Classify	Colleger	Consul	Courtesy	Crocus
Claudia	Collier	Contest	Courtier	Crœsus
Claudian	Collingwood	Context	Courtly	Cromer
Clatter	Colocynth	Contract	Courtship	Cromwell
Claymore	Colonel	Contrast	Covenant	Crony
Clearance	Colonist	Convert	Coventry	Crosspatch
Clearer	Colony	Convict	Covetous	Crochet

Crowner	Cynthia	Daring	Deftly	Dido
Crucible	Cypher	Darkie	Delaware	Difference
Cruel	Cypress	Darkly	Delegate	Diffident
Cruelty	Cyprian	Darkness	Delia	Digby
Cruiser	Cyprus	Darksome	Delicate	Digit
Crumble	Cyril	Darling	Delta	Dignity
Crumpet	Cyrus	Darlington	Deluge	Diligence
Crusty		Darnley	Democrat	Diligent
Cryer		Darter	Demon	Dimity
Crystal	Dabble	Dartmouth	Denison	Dimly
Crywell	Dabbler	Dashaway	Denizen	Dimple
Cubicle	Dabchick	Dasher	Denmark	Dinah
Cudgel	Dabster	Dashwood	Dennis	Dingle
Culpable	Dacian	Dastard	Density	Dingy
Culprit	Dactyl	Dauntless	Dentist	Diomed
Culture	Dado	David	Denton	Diplomat
Culvert	Daedalus	Dawdle	Deputy	Discipline
Cumberland	Daffodil	Dawdler	Derby	Discord
Cumbrous	Dagger	Daybreak	Derelict	Discount
Cunning	Dagmar	Daydream	Dermot	Discourse
Cupid	Dagon	Dayfly	Derogate	Dismal
Curate	Dahlia	Daylight	Dervish	Dissolute
Curdle	Daily	Daytime	Desmond	Distaff
Curfew	Daimler	Daystar	Desolate	Distance
Curio	Dainty	Dazzle	Desperate	Ditto
Curious	Dairymaid	Dazzler	Despot	Ditty
Curlew	Daisy	Deacon	Destiny	Diver
Curly	Dalesman	Deaconess	Destitute	Dividend
Currency	Dalliance	Deadlock	Detriment	Dizzy
Curzon	Damage	Deadly	Devilry	Doctor
Curtain	Damaris	Dealer	Devious	Document
Cushion	Damask	Dealing	Dewberry	Dodger
Custard	Damon	Deanery	Dewdrop	Dodo
Custody	Damper	Dearly	Dexter	Doeskin
Custom	Damsel	Deborah	Dexterous	Doleful
Customer	Damson	Debtor	Dextral	Dolesome
Cuthbert	Danceaway	Decimal	Diadem	Dollar
Cutler	Dancer	Decorate	Diagram	Dolly
Cutlass	Dandle	Dedicate	Dialect	Dolphin
Cygnet	Dandy	Deemster	Dialogue	Domicile
Cymbal	Danger	Deemstress	Diamond	Dominant
Cymric	Dangerous	Deeply	Diary	Dominic
Cynic	Daphne	Deficit	Dicebox	Domino
Cynical	Dareful	Definite	Difficult	Doncaster

Donna	Dreamless	Duster	Egret	Epilogue
Donovan	Dreamy	Dusty	Eileen	Episode
Doomsday	Dreary	Dutchman	Elcho	Epitaph
Dora	Dredger	Duteous	Eleanor	Epithet
Dorcas	Dresden	Dutiful	Elegance	Epitome
Dorimont	Dribble	Duty	Elegant	Equerry
Doris	Driblet	Dwindle	Elegy	Equinox
Dormant	Drinker	Dynamite	Element	Equity
Dormer	Drivel	Dynamo	Elevate	Erin
Dormouse	Driveller	Dynasty	Elfish	Ermine
Dorothy	Driver	Dynevor	Eloquence	Ernest
Dorset	Drizzle		Eloquent	Errand
Dotage	Drollery		Elsie	Errant
Dotterel	Drover	Eager	Elspeth	Erskine
Doublet	Drowsy	Eagle	Embassy	Escort
Doubtful	Drudgery	Eaglet	Ember	Esmond
Doughty	Drugget	Earing	Emblem	Essence
Douglas	Druggist	Earldom	Emerald	Esther
Dover	Druid	Early	Emerson	Estimate
Dowager	Drummer	Earnest	Emery	Ethel
Dowdy	Drunkard	Earthquake	Emigrant	Etheling
Downy	Dryad	Earwig	Emily	Ethelred
Downright	Dryden	Easeful	Eminence	Etiquette
Dowry	Dryly	Easily	Eminent	Eulogy
Draco	Dubia	Easter	Emma	Eustace
Dracula	Dubious	Easterly	Emperor	Eva
Draggle	Dublin	Easy	Emphasis	Eveline
Dragoman	Duchess	Ebonite	Empire	Evelyn
Dragon	Duckling	Ebony	Empress	Evening
Dragsman	Dudley	Ebor	Ena	Evenly
Dramatist	Duelist	Echo	Endive	Eventide
Drainer	Dukedom	Ecstasy	Endless	Evident
Draftsman	Dulcet	Edify	Energy	Excellent
Draper	Dulcie	Edgar	Enmity	Exeat
Drapery	Dulcimer	Edible	Ensign	Exeter
Drastic	Dumpy	Edict	Entity	Exigence
Drawback	Duncan	Edith	Enterprise	Exigent
Drayman	Dunster	Editor	Envious	Exile
Drayton	Duplex	Ednam	Envoy	Exodus
Dreadful	Duplicate	Edward	Envy	Expert
Dreadless	Durable	Effable	Epaulette	Expiate
Dreadnaught	Durance	Egbert	Epicure	Extra
Dreamer	Durity	Egerton	Epigram	Extract
Dreamland	Dusky	Egress	Epigraph	Eyebrow

Eyelash	Fanciful	Ferment	Fireman	Florid
Eyelet	Fancy	Fernery	Firequeen	Florist
	Fanfare	Ferryman	Firetail	Florizel
	Fangle	Fertile	Firmly	Flotsam
Faber	Fanny	Fervent	Firmness	Flounder
Fabian	Fantail	Fervid	Fisherman	Flourish
Fabius	Fantasy	Fervour	Fitful	Flourisher
Fable	Faraday	Festival	Fitly	Flowery
Fabric	Farcical	Festive	Fitness	Fluency
Fabulous	Farewell	Fetter	Fitzroy	Fluent
Facer	Farthing	Fettle	Fixture	Flunkey
Faction	Farmer	Fettler	Fizzer	Flurry
Factious	Farquhar	Feudal	Fizzle	Fluster
Factor	Farrier	Feverish	Flagman	Flutter
Factory	Fascinate	Fiat	Flagon	Flyaway
Faculty	Fashion	Fibre	Flagrant	Flyer
Faddist	Fatal	Fibster	Flagstaff	Foamy
Faggott	Fatalist	Fickle	Flambeau	Focus
Failure	Fateful	Fiction	Flameless	Foeman
Fairburn	Fathom	Fiddler	Flamer	Foible
Fairfax	Fatima	Fidget	Flammable	Foiler
Fairing	Faulter	Fieldfare	Flannel	Foliage
Fairlight	Faulty	Fiendish	Flapper	Folio
Fairmaid	Faustus	Fiery	Flasher	Foljamb
Fairly	Favorite	Fifer	Flatterer	Folkestone
Fairplay	Favour	Figaro	Flattery	Follower
Fairstar	Fealty	Figment	Flavia	Folly
Fairway	Fearful	Figure	Flavour	Fondle
Fairy	Fearless	Filbert	Flaxen	Foolery
Faithful	Fearnaught	Filcher	Fleecer	Foolish
Faithless	Fearsome	Filial	Fleetly	Foolscap
Falcon	Feasible	Filigree	Fleetwing	Footfall
Falconer	Feather	Fillet	Fleetwood	Footlight
Falkland	Feature	Filter	Fleshy	Footman
Fallacy	Federal	Filmy	Flexible	Footpath
Fallible	Federate	Finder	Flicker	Footprint
Falmouth	Feeble	Finery	Flightly	Footstep
Falsehood	Felix	Fingal	Flimsy	Footstool
Falstaff	Felony	Finisher	Flinger	Forage
Falter	Female	Finnikin	Flippant	Forager
Famish	Fencer	Firearm	Flora	Forceless
Famine	Fender	Firebrand	Floral	Forcer
Famous	Fenian	Firefly	Florence	Forcible
Fancier	Ferdinand	Firelock	Florian	Fordham

Forecast	Franchise	Frosty	Gabble	Garbage
Foreigner	Frankfort	Frozen	Gabbler	Garble
Foreland	Franklin	Frugal	Gabriel	Gardener
Forelock	Frankly	Fruiterer	Gadabout	Gargle
Foreman	Frantic	Fruitful	Gadfly	Gargoyle
Foremost	Fraser	Fruitless	Gaelic	Garish
Foresail	Fraudulent	Frumpy	Gaffer	Garland
Foreshaw	Freakish	Fuchsia	Gaiety	Garlic
Foresight	Freckle	Fuddle	Gaily	Garment
Forester	Frederick	Fuddler	Gainer	Garner
Foretaste	Freeborn	Fugitive	Gainful	Garnet
Forfeit	Freedom	Fugleman	Gainless	Garnish
Forfeiture	Freely	Fulbeck	Gainsay	Garrison
Forger	Freeman	Fulgent	Gains-	Garrulous
Forgery	Freestone	Fullerton	borough	Garter
Formal	Freetrade	Fulmen	Gainsome	Gasbag
Formalist	Freezer	Fulsome	Galahad	Gaslight
Formative	Frenzy	Fumble	Galaxy	Gaspar
Former	Frequence	Fumbler	Galipot	Gatherer
Formula	Frequent	Function	Gallant	Gatty
Fortescue	Fresco	Fungus	Gallery	Gaudy
Fortitude	Freshman	Funnel	Galley	Gauger
Fortress	Fretful	Funnylad	Galliard	Gauntlet
Fortunate	Fretwork	Funnylass	Gallinule	Gauzy
Fortune	Friar	Furbelow	Galloper	Gaylad
Forward	Friable	Furbish	Galloway	Gaylass
Founder	Friction	Furbisher	Galopin	Gaymaid
Foundling	Friday	Furious	Galway	Gayman
Foundress	Friendless	Furlong	Gambit	General
Foundry	Friendly	Furlough	Gambler	Generous
Fountain	Friendship	Furnace	Gambol	Genial
Fowler	Frigate	Furnish	Gameboy	Genitor
Foxglove	Frightful	Furnisher	Gamecock	Genius
Fraction	Frigid	Furrier	Gamely	Gentian
Fractious	Fringent	Furtive	Gamesome	Gentle
Fracture	Fripery	Fury	Gamester	Gentleman
Fragile	Frisky	Fusible	Gamestress	Gently
Fragment	Fritter	Fussy	Gammon	Genuine
Fragrance	Frivolous	Fustian	Gander	Genus
Fragrant	Frolic	Fustic	Ganger	Geoffrey
Frailty	Frolicsome	Futile	Gangway	Georgian
Framer	Frontage	Future	Gannet	Georgie
Framework	Frontier		Ganymede	German
Francis	Frontlet		Gaoler	Gertrude

E

Gesture	Glossary	Grafter	Groundsel	Hadrian
Ghastly	Glossy	Grafton	Grovel	Haggard
Ghostly	Gloucester	Grammer	Groveller	Haggle
Giant	Glover	Grammont	Growler	Hailstone
Giantess	Glowing	Grampian	Gruesome	Halcyon
Giddy	Glowworm	Grampus	Grumbler	Halibut
Gideon	Glutton	Granby	Grumpy	Halifax
Giggle	Gobbler	Grandison	Grunter	Halma
Gilbert	Goblet	Granville	Guardian	Halo
Gilder	Goblin	Graphic	Guardless	Halter
Gimcrack	Goddess	Grapnel	Guardsman	Halyard
Gimlet	Godfrey	Grappler	Gudgeon	Hamilton
Gipsy	Golden	Grapple	Guesswork	Hamlet
Girder	Goldfinch	Grasper	Guidance	Hammock
Girdle	Goldsmith	Grateful	Guideful	Hamper
Girlish	Golfer	Gratis	Guideless	Hampton
Girlhood	Gondola	Gratitude	Guider	Handcuff
Gladly	Goneril	Gravity	Guildford	Handful
Gladness	Goodman	Gravy	Guileless	Handglass
Gladsome	Goodness	Grayling	Guilesome	Handicap
Gladwin	Gooseberry	Grazier	Guillotine	Handicraft
Gladys	Goosecap	Greatly	Guiltless	Handel
Glamour	Goosestep	Greatorex	Guilty	Handmaid
Glancer	Gordian	Grecian	Gullet	Handrail
Glaring	Gordon	Greedy	Gulliver	Handsome
Glasgow	Gorgeous	Gregory	Gumption	Handspike
Glaucus	Gorgon	Grenadine	Gunboat	Handy
Glazier	Goshawk	Greeting	Gunner	Hangman
Gleaming	Gosling	Greta	Gunnery	Hanker
Gleaner	Gossamer	Gretna	Gunshot	Hannibal
Gleeful	Gossip	Griddle	Gunsmith	Hanover
Gleesome	Gothic	Gridiron	Gurgle	Hapless
Glenwood	Governess	Grievance	Gushing	Haply
Glibly	Governor	Grievous	Gusset	Happiness
Glider	Gownsman	Griffin	Gusty	Happy
Glimmer	Grabber	Grimly	Guzman	Harasser
Glisten	Gracecup	Grimston	Guzzler	Harbinger
Glitter	Graceful	Grinder	Gwendoline	Harborough
Gloaming	Graceless	Gristle	Gymnast	Hardship
Globule	Grachus	Grizzle		Hardware
Gloomy	Gracious	Grocer		Hardwicke
Gloria	Gradient	Grocery	Hackle	Hardy
Glorious	Gradual	Groomsman	Hackler	Harebell
Glory	Graduate	Grotto	Hackster	Haricot

Harkaway	Heathen	Hesperus	Huckster	Impulse
Harlech	Heather	Hester	Huddle	Incense
Harlequin	Hebe	Hickory	Hudibras	Incident
Harmful	Hebrew	Highflyer	Huguenot	Income
Harmless	Hecate	Highland	Humbert	Index
Harmony	Heckle	Highway-	Humble	Indian
Harold	Heckler	man	Humbug	Indigo
Harper	Hector	Hilda	Humorous	Indolence
Harpist	Hectrian	Hindrance	Humphry	Indolent
Harpsichord	Hecuba	History	Humpty	Industry
Harpy	Heedful	Holder	Hungry	Infamous
Harriet	Heedless	Holdfast	Hunter	Inference
Harrow	Heiress	Holiday	Huntly	Infinite
Hartshorn	Heirloom	Holloway	Huntress	Ingoldsby
Harvester	Helen	Holocaust	Huntsman	Injury
Hassock	Helena	Holster	Hurdle	Inkling
Hastings	Helicon	Homage	Hurricane	Inky
Hasty	Hellebore	Homeless	Hurry	Inmate
Hatchet	Helmet	Homely	Hurtful	Innocence
Hateful	Helper	Homespun	Husky	Innocent
Hatred	Helpful	Homily	Hustler	Inquest
Haughty	Helpless	Hominy	Hyacinth	Insolence
Haulage	Helpmate	Honesty	Hydrant	Insolent
Havelock	Hemlock	Honey	Hymen	Instep
Havoc	Henbane	Honeymoon	Hymnal	Instinct
Hawfinch	Henchman	Honeycomb	Hyphen	Insult
Hawker	Hengist	Hoodwink	Hypocrite	Interest
Hawthorn	Herald	Hopbine	Hyssop	Interval
Hazard	Herbage	Hopeful		Intimate
Hazardous	Herbalist	Hopeless		Intricate
Hazle	Hercules	Hornet	Ibex	Iodine
Hazlewood	Herdsman	Hornpipe	Idiom	Ireland
Hazy	Hereford	Horror	Idiot	Irksome
Headman	Heresy	Horsa	Idler	Isobel
Headlong	Heretic	Hospodar	Ignorance	Istria
Headstrong	Heriot	Hostage	Ignorant	Ivanhoe
Headway	Heritage	Hostess	Image	Ivory
Headwind	Hermit	Hostile	Immigrant	Ivy
Healthful	Hermitage	Hotspur	Imminent	
Healthy	Hero	Housemaid	Impetus	
Hearsay	Herod	Hover	Impious	Jackdaw
Heartless	Heroine	Hoyden	Impish	Jackobite
Heartsease	Hertford	Hubbub	Impudence	Jailer
Hearty	Hesper	Hubert	Impudent	Janitor

Jargon	Jumper	Ladyblush	Lazarus	Lindsay
Jarvey	Juniper	Ladylike	Lazy	Lingerer
Jasmine	Junket	Lambkin	Leader	Linguist
Jason	Jupiter	Lamprey	Leapyear	Linkboy
Jasper	Juryman	Lancaster	Lecture	Linkman
Jaunty	Justice	Lancelot	Lecturer	Linnet
Javelin	Justly	Lancer	Ledger	Lionel
Jealous	Juvenal	Lancet	Legacy	Lioness
Jealousy	Juvenile	Landlord	Legend	Lissom
Jerkin		Landmark	Legible	Listless
Jersey		Landrail	Legion	Lithia
Jessamy	Kaiser	Landscape	Leicester	Litigate
Jessica	Kama	Landseer	Leinster	Lively
Jessie	Katherine	Landsman	Leisure	Livid
Jester	Keeper	Languid	Lemon	Liza
Jewel	Keepsake	Languish	Lenient	Loadstar
Jeweller	Kennedy	Lansdowne	Lenity	Loadstone
Jewess	Kestrel	Lantern	Lettice	Loafer
Jezebel	Kettledrum	Lapidist	Leveller	Lobster
Jingle	Keynote	Lappet	Levity	Locket
Jocular	Kilworth	Lapwing	Lexicon	Locksmith
Joiner	Kindle	Larceny	Liberal	Locust
Joker	Kindly	Larkspur	Libertine	Lodger
Jollity	Kindness	Lascar	Liberty	Lofty
Jonathan	Kineton	Lasher	License	Logic
Jonquil	Kingcraft	Lashwood	Lictor	Logical
Jordan	Kingston	Latimer	Lifeboat	Loiterer
Jostle	Kinsman	Latitude	Lifeguard	Logwood
Journal	Kirtle	Laudable	Lifter	Lollypop
Journeyman	Kismet	Laughter	Lighthouse	Lonely
Journalist	Kitchener	Laundress	Lightfoot	Lonesome
Jovial	Knapsack	Laura	Lightly	Longbow
Joyful	Knavery	Laureate	Lightning	Looby
Joyless	Knicknack	Laurel	Lightsome	Loopole
Joyous	Kudos	Laurence	Likely	Lorimer
Jubilant		Lavender	Likewise	Lorna
Jubilee		Laverock	Lilac	Lotta
Judgement	Lable	Lavish	Lilian	Lottery
Judy	Labourer	Lawful	Lilly	Lottie
Juggler	Laceman	Lawless	Limerick	Lotus
Julia	Ladas	Lawrence	Limit	Lounger
Julian	Ladle	Lawsuit	Limner	Lovelace
Juliet	Lady	Lawyer	Lincoln	Lovelock
Jumble	Ladybird	Layman	Linda	Lovely

Lowlander	Magnum	Mariner	Medley	Mildew
Lowly	Magpie	Marjory	Medway	Mildred
Lowther	Maiden	Marker	Melanite	Milford
Loyal	Majesty	Marksman	Melba	Militant
Loyalist	Major	Marlborough	Melody	Milkmaid
Loyalty	Makeshift	Marmaduke	Melrose	Milliner
Lozenge	Malady	Marmion	Melton	Millrace
Lubin	Malaga	Marmora	Memnon	Millwood
Lucas	Malapert	Marmot	Memory	Mimic
Lucifer	Malaprop	Marplot	Menacer	Mindful
Luckless	Malice	Marquis	Mendicant	Miner
Lucky	Mallard	Marshal	Menial	Mineral
Lucy	Malmesbury	Martial	Mention	Mingle
Ludlow	Maltster	Martin	Mentor	Minim
Lufra	Malta	Martyr	Menu	Minion
Lullaby	Malvern	Marvel	Merchant	Minister
Lunatic	Mameluke	Marvellous	Merciful	Minster
Lurcher	Manacle	Mary	Mercury	Minstrel
Lurgan	Manager	Masher	Mercy	Minuet
Lurline	Manchester	Masker	Meredith	Minus
Lustre	Mandate	Master	Merit	Mirabel
Lustrous	Mandrake	Masterful	Merlin	Miracle
Lusty	Manfred	Matador	Mermaid	Miriam
Lutestring	Manful	Matchbox	Merman	Mirror
Luther	Mangle	Matchem	Merrimac	Mirthful
Lutterworth	Maniac	Matchless	Merriment	Mischief
Luxury	Manicure	Matress	Merryboy	Miscreant
Lydia	Manifest	Matron	Merrylass	Miser
Lynton	Manifold	Mavis	Merryman	Misery
Lyric	Mannerly	Maxim	Messenger	Missal
	Mannikin	Maximus	Messmate	Mistletoe
	Mantle	Mayday	Meteor	Mistress
Mabel	Manual	Mayflower	Method	Misty
Macaroon	Manxman	Mayfly	Mettle	Mitigant
Mackerel	Marathan	Mayoress	Mexican	Mitre
Madam	Marble	Maypole	Michael	Mixture
Madcap	Marchioness	Meantime	Microbe	Mockery
Madman	Marcia	Meanwell	Midday	Model
Madness	Marco	Measure	Middleton	Modest
Madrigal	Margaret	Medal	Midget	Modesty
Magic	Margin	Medallist	Midnight	Modish
Magical	Margot	Meddler	Midshipman	Mohawk
Magnate	Marian	Meddlesome	Midway	Mohican
Magnet	Marigold	Medium	Mighty	Moiety

Moisten	Mullet	Nebula	Nihilist	Nutmeg
Moisture	Mummer	Nebulous	Nimble	Nutriment
Moleskin	Mummery	Necklace	Nimrod	Nutshell
Molly	Mumble	Nectar	Nina	
Moment	Muniment	Nectarine	Niobe	
Momus	Munster	Nedda	Nipper	Oakham
Mona	Muriel	Needful	Nipperkin	Oarsman
Monarch	Murmur	Needless	Nitre	Oatmeal
Monastery	Murmurer	Needy	Nobbler	Obdurate
Monitor	Muscat	Negative	Noble	Object
Monody	Muscovite	Negligence	Nobleman	Obsolete
Monogram	Music	Negligent	Noiseless	Obstacle
Monstrous	Musical	Negress	Noisy	Obstinate
Monument	Musket	Negro	Nominal	Obvious
Moody	Muslin	Neighbour	Nominate	Octave
Moonbeam	Mussulman	Nelly	Nonsense	Oculist
Moonlight	Mustard	Nelson	Nonsuch	Oddity
Moonshine	Muster	Nemesis	Noonday	Odious
Moonstone	Musty	Neptune	Noontide	Officer
Moorhen	Mutiny	Nero	Norah	Offspring
Mopsy	Myra	Nervous	Norfolk	Olga
Moral	Myrtle	Nestor	Norma	Olive
Moralist	Mystery	Nettle	Normal	Oliver
Morbid	Mystic	Nettler	Norman	Omega
Morgan	Mystical	Nettleton	Norseman	Omen
Morion	Mythical	Network	Norval	Ominous
Mormon	.	Neutral	Norwood	Onslow
Morphia		Newgate	Nosegay	Onyx
Morsel	Nabob	Newport	Notable	Onward
Mortal	Nailer	Newsman	Notary	Opal
Mortgage	Nameless	Nibbler	Notice	Opera
Mortimer	Namesake	Nicety	Notion	Oppidan
Morton	Nancy	Nickle	Novel	Optimist
Mossrose	Naphta	Nickleby	Novelist	Option
Motive	Napier	Nigel	Novelty	Optional
Motley	Narrative	Niggard	Novice	Oracle
Mountebank	Naseby	Nigger	Nubia	Orator
Mournful	Nathan	Nightcap	Nugent	Orbit
Movable	Naughty	Nightingale	Nuisance	Orderly
Movement	Native	Nightgown	Nugget	Orchid
Muddle	Nautical	Nightly	Number	Ordinance
Muffler	Nautilus	Nightmare	Numeral	Organist
Mulberry	Neatness	Nightshade	Nuneham	Orgie
Mulciber	Neatly	Nightwatch	Nursling	Oriel

Orient	Pamphlet	Passionate	Pennon	Pickwick
Origin	Pancake	Passive	Penrhyn	Picture
Orkney	Pander	Passport	Pension	Piebald
Ormonde	Panic	Password	Pensioner	Piecrust
Ornament	Pannier	Pastime	Pensive	Pieman
Orphan	Panoply	Pastor	Pentacle	Piety
Orpheus	Pansy	Pastoral	Penury	Pigment
Orthodox	Panther	Pastry	Peony	Pikeman
Osborne	Pantomime	Pasty	Peppermint	Pilchard
Oscar	Papist	Patchwork	Peppery	Pilgrim
Osprey	Parable	Patent	Percival	Pilgrimage
Ostler	Parachute	Pathos	Perdita	Pillager
Ottoman	Paradigm	Pathway	Peregrine	Pilot
Outbreak	Paradox	Patience	Perfect	Pincher
Outcast	Paraffin	Patriarch	Perfidy	Pindar
Outcome	Paragon	Patrick	Perfume	Pinion
Outcry	Paragram	Patriot	Pericles	Pinnacle
Outfit	Paragraph	Patron	Perilous	Pintail
Outlaw	Parallel	Pauper	Periwig	Pioneer
Outlook	Paramount	Payment	Perjury	Pious
Outpost	Parapet	Peaceable	Perquisite	Piper
Outrage	Paraphrase	Peaceful	Perrier	Pirate
Overture	Parasite	Peacock	Pertinent	Pistol
Oxford	Parasol	Pearly	Pertly	Pitcher
Oxygen	Parchment	Pedagogue	Pessimist	Piteous
	Parcity	Pediment	Peter	Pitiful
	Pardon	Pedlar	Petersham	Pitiless
Packet	Parity	Peeler	Petrarch	Pittance
Packman	Parker	Peerage	Petrel	Pixie
Padlock	Parlance	Peeress	Petticoat	Placable
Padwick	Parliament	Peerless	Petulance	Placid
Pagan	Parody	Peevish	Petulant	Placida
Pageant	Parseer	Pegasus	Phalanx	Plaintiff
Painful	Parsley	Pelican	Phantom	Planet
Painter	Parsnip	Pembroke	Pharisee	Planter
Paladin	Parson	Penalty	Philomel	Plastic
Palafox	Partial	Penance	Phœbe	Plato
Palamon	Particle	Pendant	Phœnix	Platoff
Palatine	Partisan	Pendulum	Phosphate	Plaudit
Paleface	Partner	Penitence	Phosphorus	Plausible
Palmer	Pasha	Penitent	Phyllis	Playfair
Palmerston	Passable	Penman	Pibroch	Playful
Paltry	Passenger	Pennant	Picket	Playmate
Pamela	Passion	Penniless	Pickle	Plaything

Pleader	Portly	Prickly	Proxy	Quiver
Pleasant	Portman	Priestess	Prudence	Quotable
Pleasantry	Portrait	Primate	Prudent	Quotient
Pleasing	Portsmouth	Primer	Prudish	
Pleasure	Positive	Primitive	Ptarmigan	
Plenary	Possible	Primrose	Publican	Raceaway
Plenteous	Possum	Primula	Publisher	Racer
Plentiful	Postboy	Principal	Punctual	Rachel
Plenty	Poster	Printer	Pugilist	Racket
Pliable	Postman	Prior	Pungent	Rackety
Pliant	Postscript	Prioress	Punisher	Racy
Ploughman	Posture	Prisoner	Punster	Radial
Plover	Posy	Pristine	Purchase	Radiant
Plucky	Potent	Privilege	Puritan	Radical
Plumper	Potentate	Prizer	Purity	Radium
Plumstone	Poverty	Probity	Purple	Radius
Plunder	Powerful	Problem	Purpose	Raeburn
Plunger	Practical	Proctor	Purser	Raffle
Plutus	Practise	Prodigal	Puzzle	Raffler
Plymouth	Prattle	Prodigy	Puzzler	Rafter
Poacher	Prattler	Produce	Pygmy	Raftsman
Poet	Preacher	Profligate	Pyramid	Ragged
Poetess	Precedent	Progress		Raglan
Poetry	Precept	Project		Ragman
Policy	Precious	Prologue	Quaintness	Ragwort
Polish	Preface	Promise	Quaker	Raider
Politic	Prefect	Prompter	Quality	Railer
Polka	Prejudice	Pronoun	Quarrelsome	Raillery
Pomfret	Prelate	Prophecy	Quarry	Raiment
Pompey	Prelude	Prophet	Quarryman	Rainbow
Pompous	Premier	Prophetess	Quaver	Rajah
Ponder	Premium	Proselyte	Queencraft	Rakish
Ponsonby	President	Proserpine	Queenly	Ralliance
Pontifex	Pressman	Prosody	Querist	Rally
Pontiff	Pressure	Prospect	Querulous	Rallywood
Poplin	Prestige	Prosper	Query	Rambler
Poppy	Presto	Prosperous	Quester	Rampant
Popular	Pretext	Prosy	Question	Rampart
Porcelain	Prettylass	Protest	Quibble	Rampish
Portable	Prettyman	Protestant	Quibbler	Ramrod
Porter	Previous	Proverb	Quickly	Ramsay
Portia	Priam	Provident	Quickness	Rancour
Portion	Priceless	Provost	Quickstep	Randolph
Portland	Pricket	Prowler	Quidnunc	Random

Ranger	Rector	Resonant	Ringdove	Rookwood
Ranks-	Redcap	Respite	Ringlet	Roquelaure
borough	Redcar	Restful	Ringwood	Rory
Ransack	Reddeer	Restive	Riot	Rosa
Ransom	Redolent	Restless	Rioter	Rosabel
Rantaway	Redpath	Reticent	Riotous	Rosalind
Ranter	Redpole	Reticule	Ripple	Rosamond
Rantipole	Redrose	Retinue	Risky	Rosary
Rapid	Redshank	Reuter	Rita	Roseate
Rapier	Redskin	Revel	Ritual	Rosebery
Rapture	Redstart	Reveller	Rival	Rosebud
Rarity	Redwing	Revelry	Rivalry	Roseleaf
Rascal	Reefer	Revenue	Rivet	Rosemary
Rashness	Reflex	Reverence	Rivulet	Rosery
Rasper	Refuge	Reverie	Roaster	Rosewood
Raspberry	Regal	Rhapsody	Robber	Rostrum
Rasselas	Regan	Rhenish	Robin	Rosy
Rataplan	Regent	Rhetoric	Rocker	Rotary
Rateable	Regia	Rheumy	Rockery	Roundelay
Ratify	Regiment	Rhinewine	Rocket	Rounder
Ratio	Reginald	Rhoda	Rockingham	Rouser
Rational	Region	Rhombic	Rockwood	Rover
Rattle	Register	Rhubarb	Roderick	Rowdy
Rattlecap	Regular	Rhymer	Rodney	Roxburgh
Rattler	Regulate	Rhythm	Rodomont	Royal
Ravager	Regulus	Ribald	Roebuck	Royalist
Raven	Reindeer	Ribaldry	Roguery	Royalty
Ravenous	Relative	Ribbon	Roguish	Royston
Ravisher	Relegate	Richer	Roister	Rubens
Raymond	Relevant	Richmond	Roisterer	Rubican
Readily	Relic	Riddance	Rokeby	Rubicund
Ready	Relish	Riddle	Roland	Rubio
Reaper	Remedy	Ridicule	Rollick	Rubric
Reason	Remnant	Ridley	Roma	Ruby
Reasoner	Remus	Riffraff	Roman	Ruction
Rebel	Render	Rifleman	Romeo	Ruddy
Rebus	Renegade	Rifler	Romney	Rudiment
Recent	Renovate	Righteous	Romper	Rueful
Reckless	Rental	Rightful	Rompish	Ruffian
Reckoner	Reprimand	Rigid	Romulus	Rufford
Recompense	Reprobate	Rigmarole	Rona	Ruffle
Record	Rescue	Rigorous	Ronald	Ruffler
Recreant	Resident	Rigour	Ronda	Rufus
Rectitude	Resolute	Rimy	Rookery	Rugged

F

Ruin	Sally	Saxon	Seamstress	Shakspeare
Ruinous	Salvage	Scamper	Searcher	Shameful
Ruler	Salvo	Scamperdale	Seaweed	Shameless
Ruminate	Sameness	Scampish	Secrecy	Shamrock
Rummager	Sample	Scandal	Secret	Shapeless
Rumour	Sampler	Scandelous	Secretary	Shapely
Rumple	Samson	Scanty	Sedulous	Sharper
Rumpus	Sanction	Scaraben	Seemly	Shaver
Rumsey	Sanctuary	Scarborough	Seeker	Sheba
Runagate	Sanctum	Scarcity	Seldom	Sheeny
Runaway	Sandal	Scarlet	Selfish	Shekel
Rundle	Sandiway	Scathless	Selim	Shelagh
Rupert	Sandon	Scattercash	Selima	Sheldrake
Rural	Sandow	Scavenger	Selvedge	Shelter
Rushlight	Sandstone	Scenery	Senator	Shepherdess
Russet	Sandwich	Sceptic	Seneschal	Sherbrooke
Rustic	Sandy	Sceptical	Senior	Sheridan
Rustica	Sanford	Sceptre	Senseless	Sheriff
Rusticus	Sanguine	Schemer	Sensible	Sherry
Rustler	Santa	Scholar	Sensitive	Shiftless
Rusty	Sanity	Schoolboy	Sentence	Shifty
Ruthful	Sapient	Schoolgirl	Sentient	Shiner
Ruthless	Sapper	Schooner	Sentiment	Shootaway
Rutland	Sapphire	Science	Sentinel	Shooter
	Sappho	Scientist	Sentry	Shoveller
	Saraband	Scoffer	Sepia	Shuffler
Sabine	Saracen	Scornful	Sepoy	Shylock
Sable	Sarah	Scorpion	Sequel	Sibyl
Sabre	Sarcenet	Scotchman	Sequence	Sideral
Sackbut	Satchel	Scotland	Sequin	Sifter
Sackcloth	Satellite	Scoundrel	Serfdom	Sightly
Sacrifice	Satin	Scrambler	Sergeant	Sigma
Safeguard	Satire	Scrawler	Serial	Signal
Safety	Satirist	Screamer	Series	Signet
Saffron	Satrap	Scribbler	Serious	Silence
Sago	Saturn	Scrimmager	Sermon	Silent
Sailor	Saucebox	Scripture	Servia	Silica
Sainfoin	Saucy	Scrivener	Servitor	Silkworm
Saintly	Saunter	Scruple	Settler	Silky
Saladin	Saunterer	Scrupulous	Sexton	Silva
Salary	Savage	Scrutiny	Sextant	Silvery
Salesman	Savant	Sculptor	Seymour	Silvia
Salient	Savory	Sealskin	Shadow	Silvio
Salisbury	Sawyer	Seaman	Shaker	Simnel

Simon	Social	Speedwell	Starlight	Strategy
Simper	Socialist	Speedy	Starling	Stratum
Simple	Soda	Spencer	Starter	Strawberry
Simpleton	Sofa	Spendthrift	Startle	Streamer
Simplify	Softly	Spicy	Stately	Streamlet
Sinbad	Solace	Spider	Statement	Strenuous
Sinecure	Soldier	Spindle	Statesman	Strickland
Sinful	Solitude	Spinner	Stationer	Strident
Singer	Solomon	Spinster	Statue	Striker
Singwell	Solon	Spiteful	Stature	Stringent
Sinister	Soluble	Spitfire	Status	Stringer
Sinless	Somerset	Splendid	Steadfast	Striper
Sinner	Songbird	Splendour	Steady	Stripling
Sintram	Songster	Spillikin	Stealthy	Striver
Siphon	Songstress	Spinaway	Stella	Stroker
Sirius	Songtag	Splinter	Stentor	Stroller
Skater	Sonnet	Spoiler	Sterling	Struggler
Skilful	Sophie	Spokesman	Sternly	Student
Skipper	Sorcerer	Sponsor	Steward	Studious
Skirmish	Sorceress	Sporran	Stewardess	Stumpy
Skirmisher	Sorcery	Sportful	Stickler	Sturdy
Skittish	Sorrowful	Sportive	Stigma	Stylish
Skylark	Souvenir	Sportly	Stilton	Suavity
Skylight	Sovereign	Sportsman	Stimulant	Subaltern
Slander	Spacious	Spotless	Stimulous	Subject
Slapdash	Spangle	Sprightful	Stinger	Subsidy
Slasher	Spaniard	Sprightly	Stingo	Substance
Slavery	Spanker	Springer	Stipend	Substantive
Sleepy	Sparkle	Sprinkle	Stipulate	Substitute
Slender	Sparkler	Squadron	Stiver	Subterfuge
Sligo	Sparkling	Squeezer	Stockdove	Subtlety
Slipaway	Sparksman	Squibbler	Stoic	Succour
Slipper	Spartan	Squatter	Stoker	Succulent
Slumber	Speaker	Stafford	Stormer	Suffrage
Smartly	Special	Staidly	Stormont	Suitable
Snasher	Specify	Stainless	Stormy	Suitor
Smiler	Specimen	Stalker	Story	Suleiman
Smoker	Specious	Stalwart	Straggler	Sulky
Smuggler	Speckle	Stamford	Straightway	Sullivan
Smutty	Spectacle	Stammerer	Stranger	Sulphur
Snatcher	Spectrum	Stamper	Strapper	Sultan
Snowball	Specular	Standard	Strapping	Sultry
Snowdrop	Speculum	Stanley	Stratagem	Summary
Sociable	Speechless	Stanza	Strategist	Summit

Summons	Sylvan	Tangler	Temperate	Thrasher
Sumptuous	Sylvia	Tankard	Tempest	Thrifty
Sunbeam	Symbol	Tanner	Templar	Thrilling
Sunderland	Symmetry	Tantalize	Temporal	Throstle
Sundown	Sympathy	Tantalus	Tempter	Thruster
Sundry	Symphony	Tantivy	Temptress	Thunder
Sunlight	Symptom	Tantrum	Tenable	Thunderbolt
Sunny	Syndic	Tanzy	Tenant	Thunderer
Sunray	Syndicate	Taper	Tendency	Ticket
Sunrise	Syntax	Tapestry	Tender	Tickford
Sunset	Syren	Tapster	Tenderness	Tickle
Sunshade	Syrian	Tardy	Tendril	Tickler
Sunshine	System	Target	Tennyson	Ticklish
Sunstroke		Tariff	Tension	Tidings
Super		Tarlatan	Tentative	Tidy
Supple	Tablet	Tarnish	Tenuous	Tiffany
Suppliant	Tabloid	Tarquin	Termagant	Tiger
Surety	Taciturn	Tarrogan	Terminal	Tigress
Surgeon	Tackler	Tartan	Terrapin	Tilter
Surly	Tactic	Tartar	Terrible	Timbrel
Surplice	Tactless	Tartly	Terror	Timely
Surrogate	Taffeta	Tassel	Tester	Timid
Susan	Taffy	Tasteful	Testy	Timon
Sutton	Tagus	Tasty	Tetrarch	Timorous
Swagger	Tailor	Tattle	Textile	Timothy
Swallow	Taintless	Tattler	Texture	Tincture
Swanlike	Talbot	Tauntress	Thaldrom	Tinder
Swarthy	Talent	Taurus	Thankful	Tingle
Sweeper	Talisman	Tawdry	Thankless	Tinker
Sweetbread	Talkative	Tawny	Thatcher	Tinkle
Sweetest	Talker	Teacher	Theodore	Tinman
Sweetheart	Tallage	Tearful	Theorist	Tinsel
Sweetly	Tally	Tearless	Theory	Tippet
Sweetmeat	Tamable	Teasel	Thesis	Tippler
Swiftly	Tamarin	Teaser	Thespis	Tipster
Swindler	Tamarind	Technic	Thetis	Tipsy
Swinger	Tamarisk	Technical	Thievish	Tiptoe
Swivel	Tambour	Tedious	Thimble	Tiptop
Swooper	Tamerlane	Telegram	Thinker	Tiresome
Swordsman	Tamper	Telegraph	Thriftless	Tissue
Sybil	Tancred	Telephone	Thirsty	Titan
Sycamore	Tangent	Telescope	Thistle	Titian
Sycophant	Tangible	Telltale	Thoughtful	Title
Syllable	Tangle	Temeraire	Thoughtless	Titmouse

Titus	Tracker	Trespasser	Truthful	Universe
Toady	Trackless	Trial	Trywell	Uppish
Toffee	Tractable	Tribune	Tudor	Uproar
Toiler	Tractor	Tribute	Tulip	Upset
Toilet	Trader	Trickery	Tumbler	Upshot
Toilsome	Tradesman	Trickster	Tumult	Upstart
Token	Traffic	Trickstress	Tunable	Urchin
Tolerant	Tragedy	Tricksy	Tuneful	Urgent
Tomahawk	Tragic	Tricolor	Tuner	Uriel
Tomboy	Trailer	Trident	Tunic	Ursula
Tomtom	Trainer	Trifle	Turban	Useful
Tonic	Traitor	Trifler	Turbulent	Usher
Tonsure	Trajan	Trilby	Turmoil	Usurer
Tontine	Trammel	Trimbush	Turncoat	Usury
Tony	Trampler	Trimmer	Turnstile	Utterance
Toothsome	Tranquil	Trimming	Turpin	
Topaz	Transcript	Trinket	Turquoise	
Toper	Transept	Triton	Tuscan	Vacancy
Topic	Transfer	Tripaway	Tutor	Vacant
Topical	Transient	Triplet	Twilight	Vagabond
Topmost	Transit	Tripod	Twinker	Vagrant
Topper	Transom	Tripos	Twinkle	Valda
Topsail	Transport	Triumph	Twister	Valentine
Topsy	Trapper	Trivial	Typical	Valesman
Topthorn	Trappist	Trojan	Tyranny	Valet
Torchlight	Traveller	Trophy	Tyrant	Valiant
Torment	Traverser	Tropical	Tyro	Valid
Torpid	Treacherous	Trotwood		Valorous
Torrent	Treachery	Troubadour		Valour
Tortuous	Treacle	Troubler	Ugly	Valuable
Torture	Treason	Troublesome	Uhlan	Value
Torturer	Treasure	Trouncer	Ulster	Vampire
Tory	Treasurer	Truant	Ultimate	Vanadis
Total	Treatise	Truckler	Umber	Vanda
Touching	Treaty	Trueboy	Umbrage	Vandal
Touchstone	Treble	Truelass	Umpire	Vandyke
Touchwood	Trefoil	Truelove	Una	Vanguard
Tourist	Trembler	Truemaid	Unicorn	Vanish
Tournament	Tremor	Trueman	Uniform	Vanity
Townsman	Tremulo	Trumpery	Union	Vanquish
Towser	Tremulous	Trumpeter	Unionist	Vanquisher
Tozer	Trencher	Truro	Unison	Vantage
Tracer	Trepid	Trustful	Unit	Vapid
Tracery	Trespass	Trusty	Unity	Vapour

Variance	Versatile	Visitor	Wanton	Webster
Variant	Version	Vista	Warble	Wedgewood
Various	Vertical	Vistula	Warbler	Wedlock
Varlet	Vesper	Vital	Warcry	Welcome
Varna	Vesta	Vivian	Warden	Welfare
Varnish	Vestal	Vivid	Warfare	Welkin
Varsity	Vestige	Vixen	Warily	Welladay
Vary	Vestris	Vizier	Warlaby	Wellington
Vassal	Vesture	Vocal	Warlike	Welshman
Vatican	Veteran	Vocalist	Warlock	Welter
Vaulter	Veto	Volatile	Warpaint	Wenlock
Vaultress	Vexer	Volley	Warranty	Wentworth
Vaunter	Viceroy	Voltigeur	Warrener	Westbury
Veda	Vicious	Voluble	Warrior	Westward
Vehement	Victim	Volume	Warspite	Wexford
Vellum	Victor	Voluntary	Warwick	Whalebone
Velvet	Victory	Vortex	Wary	Whatnot
Venal	Victress	Votary	Washington	Wheedle
Vendor	Vigil	Voter	Waspish	Whetstone
Venerable	Vigilance	Voucher	Wasteful	Whiffler
Venery	Vigilant	Vowel	Watchful	Whimper
Vengeance	Vigorous	Voyager	Watchman	Whimsey
Vengeful	Viking	Vulcan	Watchword	Whimsical
Venial	Villager	Vulpine	Waterford	Whipcord
Venice	Villain	Vulture	Waterman	Whippy
Venison	Vincent		Waterloo	Whipster
Venom	Vincible		Waterwitch	Whirligig
Venomous	Vinery	Wafer	Watkin	Whirlpool
Venture	Vineyard	Wafter	Wavelet	Whirlwind
Venturer	Vintage	Waggery	Waver	Whisker
Venturous	Vinter	Waggoner	Waverer	Whisky
Venus	Viola	Wagtail	Waverley	Whisper
Vera	Violate	Waister	Waxwork	Whisperer
Verbal	Violence	Waitress	Waxy	Whistler
Verdant	Violent	Wakefield	Wayfare	Whitaker
Verderer	Violet	Wakeful	Wayward	Whitby
Verdict	Virgil	Wallflower	Wealthy	Whitebait
Verdure	Virgin	Wallace	Wearisome	Whiteboy
Verger	Virtue	Wallop	Weary	Whiteleaf
Verily	Virtuous	Walter	Weasel	Whitethroat
Veritas	Virulent	Wamba	Weather-	Whitewash
Verity	Viscount	Wanderer	gauge	Whittington
Vernal	Visible	Wansford	Weathercock	Whynot
Vernon	Vision	Wantage	Weaver	Wicker

Wicket	Windward	Wolfish	Worthless	Yeoman
Wicklow	Winifred	Wolsey	Worthy	Yokel
Wideawake	Winipeg	Wonder	Wrangle	Yorker
Widgeon	Winkle	Wonderful	Wrangler	Youngster
Widower	Winsome	Wondrous	Wrathful	Youthful
Wigwam	Winter	Woodbine	Wrecker	Yucca
Wildair	Winterton	Woodcock	Wrestler	Yuletide
Wildboy	Wintry	Woodcraft	Wriggle	
Wilderness	Wiry	Woodlark	Wrinkle	
Wildfire	Wisdom	Woodman	Writer	
Wildflower	Wiseacre	Woodnote	Wrongful	Zadkiel
Wildman	Wiseman	Wood-	Wryneck	Zanczic
Wilfred	Wishful	nymph	Wyvern	Zealot
Wilful	Wishwell	Worcester		Zealous
William	Wistful	Workable		Zebra
Willing	Witchcraft	Worker	Yachtsman	Zenith
Wily	Witchery	Workman	Yankee	Zephyr
Wimble	Witless	Worldly	Yarborough	Zero
Windermere	Witness	Wormwood	Yardarm	Zetland
Windfall	Wizard	Worry	Yarmouth	Zigzag
Windlass	Woeful	Worship	Yarrow	Zodiac
Windsor	Woldsman	Worshipper	Yashmak	Zulu

LONDON : VINTON & CO., LTD., 8, BREAM'S BUILDINGS, CHANCERY LANE, E.C.

Lightning Source UK Ltd.
Milton Keynes UK
175094UK00001B/1/A